"Harvesting And Using Dandelions"
For Everything From Medicine To Lotions

© Connie McCauley 2018, All rights Reserved

Disclaimer

The author has made every attempt to be as accurate and complete as possible in the creation of this publication/PDF, however he / she **does not warrant or represent at any time that the contents within are accurate due to the rapidly changing nature of the Internet.** The author assumes no responsibility for errors, omissions, or contrary interpretation of the subject matter herein. Any perceived slights of specific persons, peoples, or organizations other published materials are unintentional and used solely for educational purposes only.

This information is not intended for use as a source of legal, business, accounting or financial advice. All readers are advised **to seek services of competent professionals in the legal, business, accounting, health, dietary and finance field.** No representation is made or implied that the reader will do as well from using the suggested techniques, strategies, methods, systems, or ideas; rather it is presented for news value only.

The author does not assume any responsibility or liability **whatsoever** for what you choose to do with this information. Use your own judgment. Consult appropriate professionals before starting a business or making ANY investment. Any perceived remark, comment or use of organizations, people mentioned and any resemblance to characters living, dead or otherwise, real or fictitious does not mean that they support this content in any way but is provided for news value / information only.

There are no guarantees of accuracies or health benefits. Readers are asked to consult their doctor and other medical professionals before changing their diet or consuming any foods based on this guide.

Readers are cautioned to rely on their own judgment about their individual circumstances to act accordingly. By reading any document, the reader agrees that under no circumstances is the author responsible for any losses, direct or indirect, that are incurred as a result of use of the information contained within this document, including - but not limited to errors, omissions, or inaccuracies.

© 2018 Harvesting And Using Dandelions For Everything From Medicine To Lotions by Connie McCauley, All Rights Reserved.

Contents

Disclaimer 2
Introduction **5**
    Botanical Run Down 7
Why Natural Matters **9**
    Fabulous Health Benefits 11
Plant Harvesting **12**
    Making Dandelion Tea 14
    Homesteading and Foraging 15
Dandelion Root **17**
    Harvesting The Roots 19
    Dandelion Coffee 21
    Dandelion Infused Oil 22
        Infused Oil Shopping List 25
Power Juices **26**
    Dandelion Lemonade 28
    Dandelion Cordial 29
Wines and Mead **30**
    Dandelion Vinegar 31
    Dandelion Mead 32
    Dandelion Beer 34
    Dandelion Wine 37
Jams & Jellies **39**

Creative Foods **42**
    Dandelion Vanilla Cookies 43
Dandelion Lotions & Salves **44**
    Other Useful Info About Soap Making 46
    Dandelion Lavender Soap 48
    Dandelion Jojoba Soap 50
        Shopping List For Soap Making 51
    Dandelion Skin Lotion-Bars 52
    Dandelion Lip Balm 53
    Dandelion Hand Lotion 54
Final Thoughts **56**
    Stay Updated On New Books 58

Introduction

"You fight dandelions all weekend, and late Monday afternoon there they are, pert as all get out, in full and gorgeous bloom, pretty as can be, thriving as only dandelions can in the face of adversity". -Hal Borland

The humble dandelion has poems written about it and children make wishes upon the seed pods. The best part about Dandelions is their magical healing properties which most of humanity is simply unaware of.

Most people see these special little plants as weeds to be removed from lawns, when in actual fact they are one of the most important plants for someone to grow from a medicinal perspective. Before doctors took medicine to the modern level it is now, wise women were healing their communities with salves, teas and lotions made from dandelions picked from under fence posts.

Throughout this book I will educate you on some of the amazing things the humble dandelion can do to heal our body. Many people also believe the taste of the dandelion flower leans more toward honey, so how bad could it be to create homemade foods that actually taste healthy and are healthy for our body?

For too long humanity has been relying on medicines made from synthetics and other additives. Many of the medicines on the Rx market do not cure our diseases but in fact create secondary illnesses over time. With over 100,000 people each year dying from pharmaceutical medicines, isn't it time humanity considered going back to more natural plant based extracts for healing and improving our health?

Most of us have forgotten that for many decades our grandparents and great grandparents were believers in natural medicines and they harvested everything they needed to feel well, directly off the land.

The problem we are having in our modern society with herbs lies directly with a lack of education. So if your purpose in reading this book is to find more information about baking dandelion cookies or creating a skin care lotion, I am happy to show you simple recipes that can make a big difference in your lifestyle.

I can also show you how this plant can be added into all kinds of ingredients to make other things like soap. For anyone who suffers from eczema or frequent skin rashes, were you aware that dandelion soap can soothe itchy sore skin? The soap is also gentle enough to use on baby's delicate skin, so it's really worth reading some of the homemade recipes in this book.

So pull up a comfy chair and let's discuss dandelions because I have so much amazing information to share with you!

Botanical Run Down

Many of the plants once gathered for medicines came from the forests and fields where skilled healers gathered all kinds of botanicals. Dandelions are amazing healing plants that most of us can ingest and also use in other foods like nectars, wines, cakes, skin lotions and salves.

Dandelion stands out on its own because the entire plant can be consumed in one way or the other. This plant was literally the late comer in the way of healing and wasn't added into medicines until the 7th Century by Chinese Herbalists.

English doctors didn't know anything about dandelions until the 14th Century but once they were aware of the healing properties, dandelions became one of the best ways to treat people with muscle and joint pain.

The official botanical name for dandelion is Taraxacum officinale. The name Taraxacum means it was used officially in pharmacopeia as medicine for multiple human illnesses.

The plant can be grown in full sun and partial shade. Dandelion is not particular about the type of soil it grows in and the plant can also handle rougher dryer conditions as it doesn't need a lot of water to thrive. It will grow up to 24 inches high while insects like bees and ladybugs help to pollinate.

The growing Zone for dandelions is 3 to 9 so just about anyone can produce this plant in a wide range of conditions. The plant will sprout from seed in conditions as low as 50 degrees but the seeds are more likely to germinate in the mid 70's.

Dandelions can be grown indoors in pots or out in the garden, so anyone can raise a few plants for salads or medicines. If you live in an apartment complex you can still grow a few happy dandelions on a sunny windowsill and they will thrive.

If you want to use a fertilizer, I would recommend an organic brand like 'Happy Frog' which doesn't have an abundance of phosphates in it. Fish emulsion is also another good alternative fertilizer that can be added into water and diluted down.

Considering dandelions grow along roadsides they do not require a lot of gardening attention, so for busy people growing some of these plants would be ideal and no green thumb is required.

I have supplied a link to a couple of websites for anyone who wants to try their hand at growing dandelions from seed.

Source: https://homeguides.sfgate.com/grow-dandelions-indoors-pots-98287.html

Source: https://www.bookstore.ksre.ksu.edu/pubs/mf2613.pdf

In the next section of the book I go over why using natural plants like dandelions in medicines has better long term health benefits over a Rx prescription which only Band-Aid the problem.

Why Natural Matters

"It gives one a sudden start in going down a barren, stoney street, to see upon a narrow strip of grass, just within the iron fence, the radiant dandelion, shining in the grass, like a spark dropped from the sun". -Henry Ward Beecher

There was once a time when using homemade natural oils, lotions and plant based medicines was all there was. Our grandparents were harvesters and collectors of plants, oils and animal fat used to create soaps, oils and salves. Our ancestors knew how to create natural lotions and shampoos that most of us in this modern society can only imagine doing for ourselves.

Take Chinese medicines for instance, they have been known for hundreds of years as some of the most effective and long lasting cures in the world. Even now many families in the Asian Pacific region still trust Shamans and herbal healers over modern medicine.

Once upon a time, western educated doctors encouraged patients to use alternative medicines because they knew the power of Mother Nature. Medical Universities used to teach doctors the power of combining natural ingredients with other prescriptions and now young doctors only prescribe what the pharmaceutical companies teach them. They know virtually nothing about herbal remedies or their amazing healing properties.

Large Rx Corporations and skin care Companies fill their products with synthetic ingredients and chemical additives which also makes them cheap to produce. Chemicals in food, water and lotions are responsible for an increase in allergies, skin rashes and other health issues. Chemically based personal care products have questionable ingredients in them, such as parabens.

"Parabens are known endocrine disruptors that can mimic estrogen in the body. Several studies have shown that parabens can affect the mechanisms of normal breast cells and potentially influence their abnormal growth, leading to increased risk for breast cancer."

Source: https://www.bcpp.org/resource/parabens/

We were once people who trusted more in nature than we did in corporation medicine. Plant based lotions and soaps made from dandelions, offer a healthy alternative to chemically based products, which are not good for the skin, hair and body.

Throughout this book I will show you some of the alternative products you can make from Dandelions most people may not have considered before.

Fabulous Health Benefits

In this section I thought we could quickly go over the mineral content found in Dandelions along with its fantastic antioxidant properties. Because dandelion leaves are dark green in color, they contain antioxidants such as chicoric acid, luteolin, monocaffeyltartaric acid, and phenylpropanoids. Natural ingredients like these help us fight off free radicals in the body.

Young dandelion leaves contain high Beta-carotene levels along with medium levels of Vitamin E, riboflavin, ascorbic acid, calcium and iron. Each leaf contains approximately 2.1% of protein along with traces of folic acid. This plant is packed with nutrition and health.

Some of the amazing health benefits someone may experience eating dandelion leaves are:

- Lowered blood pressure

- Better control over blood sugar levels

- Reduced inflammation on sore muscles and joints

- Reduces cancer cells for the liver, colon and pancreas

- The chlorogenic acid helps in weight loss

- Protects liver tissue from toxic substances found in our environment

Plant Harvesting

"Some people need flowers, some people need dandelions. It's medicine, it's what you need at that time in your life". -Sandra Cisneros

You may have already decided to grow, harvest and use dandelions in your diet, which is a fantastic move toward cheap greens and creating healthy foods. Dandelions can replace many salad greens and are a lot healthier in their natural raw state when consumed.

Once in America, having a backyard vegetable patch with dandelions growing all over the place was a common sight because during times of war, food was hard to come by. Most people grew backyard gardens filled with all kinds of herbs out of necessity and for homemade medicines. Growing food and herbs was an essential part of life, especially if you wanted to eat healthy greens and fruits during the long winter months.

Pickling and canning food also became very popular during the war years and whole communities were deeply involved in working together. Root cellars and community buildings were often filled with bottled garden produce. To see dried plants and herbs hanging upside down on balconies and in pantries was considered normal.

When harvesting dandelions I recommend people harvest the entire dandelion plant and not just the flowers because the root is one of the most important aspects of the plant. I also recommend people use a long nosed weed-stick and pull the entire plant out. Before using any dandelion flowers check for the following:

- Bugs and other residues

- Never pick dandelions that grow close to main highways, roadsides or near industrial areas. The chemicals on these plants could be high and therefore not recommended for human consumption.

- The best time to pick the flowers is on a warm sunny day. By mid afternoon the flowers are fully open, which means any moisture on the flower has dissipated. Picking a dry flower is recommended.

- Keep picked flowers out of plastic containers. They may sweat and lose the plant value.

- Let the dandelion dry naturally by laying the flowers out on a screen or dry cloth, the air will do the rest. Don't pile all the plants together but rather spread them out evenly.

Making Dandelion Tea

Part of the harvesting process of dandelions, includes the preservation of flowers and leaves for herbal teas. I am going to include the process of drying out the plant which is a fairly simple process to follow.

Note: If you have a better way to dry out these flowers, please follow what works best for you. These are just my general guidelines.

- Placing the dandelions out on a large cloth or putting them on a large flat tray in the sun, will dry them out without damaging the petals.

- You will notice the flowers folding up and the petals will look dry when they have been sun dried.

- When over drying has occurred, the dandelion flowers and leaves look crispy. Bring the flowers inside immediately because you are now ready to make tea, soaps, oils and salves out of them.

- You can mix dandelion flowers with different green and black teas of your choice. It makes for a lovely breakfast blend or a vibrant herbal tea.

- Dandelion flowers can be added in with other flowers and fruit peels like orange. This gives teas and a tangy flavorful blend that many people enjoy.

Homesteading and Foraging

For people who are interested in homesteading, learning to harvest and forage natural plants will literally save money at the grocery store and maybe even your life one day.

It's been very sad to see how big agriculture farms took over local neighborhood farms and grew huge amounts of GMO in place of organic foods. It seems we have forgotten about our natural connection to food and that needs to be revitalized once more. Poor food choices are also a big reason why we see a lot of people wanting to leave society and go back to farming on small acre lots.

With modern medicine and chemical corporations now working together, it seems technology, science and medical splicing of genes in our food has now come to fruition.

The good news is once you learn how much can be eaten off the land, it's easy enough to grow things like wild patches of dandelions and let them take over areas where no grass is growing. Best of all you don't have to be an expert gardener to grow this plant either but the nutritional - medicinal value alone, makes the dandelion a must on the homesteading plant growing list.

Learning about the local wildlife in your area will give you the following education:

- It will teach you more about local plant life, foraging skills and the nutritional value of edible plants.

- Learning more about the local wild plants may come in handy one day and save someone's life. Many of the ancient people knew the natural bounty that came off the land, so there's no reason why we can't learn the same knowledge skills again.

- Generational education is what our planet needs more of. So when you forage encourage your children to pick plants with you. Start with something fun like wild berry picking.

- Learn the shapes and sizes of leaves that are edible from the forest. It might be a good idea to invest in a local field guide of the fauna and take that book with you wherever you go.

- Dandelions can grow in fairly harsh conditions and can be recognized by their bright yellow flowers. If you are out driving around and see some dandelions along a fence line, or in a field stop the car and pick a few. Foraging also means taking advantage of unexpected opportunities when they present themselves to us.

- I always take a bucket, some gardening gloves and a weed stick with me in the car now. I have missed so many amazing opportunities to forage that I keep a small amount of equipment with me at all times now.

- Homesteading and foraging means you are living naturally and simply off the land. Your connection to the earth will make you appreciate the bounty this planet offers to us every day.

Dandelion Root

"Dandelions, like all things in nature are beautiful when you take the time to pay attention to them." - June Stoyer

There are all kinds of herbal treatments that can be made to relieve pain or treat internal health issues. Dandelions offer numerous benefits to our internal health as well to our skin and muscles. In this section of the book I am going to discuss the importance of keeping some dandelion root on hand at all times.

The root can be dried out and used in salves and teas. Dandelion root tea can help ease swollen joint and arthritic pain, while other people will drink the tea to help purify and detox the bloodstream.

For people who have issues with their gall bladder or have bladder health issues and stomach problems, dandelion can help repair damage done to our bodies through the oxidation process.

Dandelion root also supports good liver health and detoxifies the bloodstream which reduces oxidation levels in the human body.

I am not a medical professional and the information I am supplying in this book, is for educational purposes only, please read the disclaimer in the front of this book for further information.

Most people are not aware the entire dandelion plant is edible as well as being able to create just about anything you need for cracked dry skin.

Were you aware that dark green leafy plants are the most nutritional to consume? As I previously mentioned the leaves are high in mineral and vitamin content, so they make ideal salad veggies.

The seeds from the older dandelion flowers can be harvested which means you will be able to grow more plants over time and I can literally see how growing dandelions inside the home, could end up being essential for human health at some point. With constant toxic residue in our sky from chemtrails, it just makes sense to grow more veggies in a greenhouse environment or along sunny windowsills inside the home.

Up until WW2 people were still eating dandelion leaves in place of lettuce and other salad greens. The leaves were actually more popular leaves to consume at the dinner table over other veggies like cabbage or spinach.

Nature has provided us an amazing plant filled with nutrition and natural cures and dandelions can provide health benefits that humanity needs more of than ever before.

Harvesting The Roots

"Drinking roasted dandelion root tea may be beneficial for coffee lovers who are trying to cut down their caffeine intake. It tastes relatively similar to coffee but provides better health benefits."

Source: https://articles.mercola.com/teas/dandelion-tea.aspx

In the State of Colorado there are still counties who encourage residents to eat dandelions rather than using any kind of herbicide to get rid of them. As a matter of fact in some of these counties it's actually against the law to use herbicides and why they are encouraging people to eat the dandelions instead of poisoning the environment.

Relearning some of grandma's old cures is something people should consider doing once more. Our grandparents knew a lot about the local plant life and our relatives lived long lives too. Living to the ripe old age of 90 years was fairly common once but nowadays if someone makes it to 75 we are amazed and grateful.

However it does seem like the tide of human consciousness is changing, as more people are researching alternative ways of living for optimum health.

- Dandelions make a great homemade soap, which can be done cheaply. Items for creating the soap can be easily found in thrift stores.

- Dandelion salves can also be used to help people who suffer from arthritis, inflammation and other dry skin issues.

- Dandelion teas are also extremely healthy to consume.

- When harvesting the dandelion root, try not to damage any part of it. I suggest people use a weed stick. It can be pushed into the ground and safely remove the whole plant.

- Once the root has been cleaned off, it can then be added into stews or dried out and used for other purposes.

I really recommend investing in a dehydrator and have used one myself for many years now. I dry all kinds of things like fruits and veggies and it has been a much used kitchen tool, so your initial investment will take you a long way.

Drying Dandelion Root Out

Cut the root up into long strips and then again into quarter sections. If the root strips are fairly even, a dehydrator will dry out them out in about one hour. Place the root on the dehydrator (95 Degrees Fahrenheit or 35 Degrees Celsius) for uniform drying or until the root easily snaps when drying has completed.

If you prefer not to use a dehydrator you can of course sun-dry the roots which will take 3 to 4 days for them to become brittle.

Store in a container where moisture will not rot the root.

Dandelion Coffee

As I previously mentioned in the last section of the book, dandelion root can be made into coffee and it actually tastes a lot like regular coffee beans.

Some people cannot have coffee beans in their diet as it upsets their stomach, so for these people Dandelion root coffee is a natural alternative.

How To Make Dandelion Coffee

- If you have already dried out the root, then cut the roots into very small pieces approximately 1/8th to ¼ inch across.

- Get out a medium to large roasting pan and bake the root for approximately 3.5 to 4 hours in a warm oven 210 Deg F (93 deg C). Take the root out of the oven occasionally and stir so as not to burn. When the root is finished cooking, it should be browned and completely dried out. Cool the roots down before using.

- Grind up the roots in the same way you would grind a coffee bean. Store Dandelion coffee grounds, in an airtight container until needed.

- Put 6 tablespoons of ground Dandelion root in 16 oz of boiling hot water and leave sit for 30 minutes. Reheat to desired temperature when needed. You can also add in milk and honey for taste if you wish.

Dandelion Infused Oil

Dandelion oil can have amazing health benefits on the human body. It's not just one of those oils you add to a recipe here and there either but rather a product you can use for the rest of your life.

Dandelion infused oil can also replace other oils you may be more accustomed to using like olive oil. The health benefits alone make this dandelion infused oil an important one for all kinds of treatments:

- **For first aid purposes** dandelion oil can be used on cuts, scrapes, burns and bug bites. Dandelion Infused oil will reduce aggravated and itchy areas on the surface of the skin.

- **In dry and cold conditions** dandelion oil can be used on the face and lips to prevent dry cracked skin. Infused dandelion oil is becoming a more popular ingredient in the creation of lip balms, lotions and soaps because it soothes.

- **As a sore muscle rub** where essential oils are combined together in a dandelion salve. Eucalyptus oil, tea tree, black pepper, copaiba, and lavender are all good choices for relaxing tired and sore muscles

The infused oil recipe I am providing will come in handy for cooking, skin and hair treatments. Many of homemade salves and soap recipes will require oils like olive oil, jojoba, or something similar in the mixing process.

I highly recommend having premade infusion oil always on hand, as this will cut down on time where other homemade recipes call for it.

Other things you will need to make the oil

1. You will need a burner or stove.
2. Two glass jars that can hold up to 12 to 15oz of fluid. *A sealed jar like a mason jar or twist top jar will work*
3. Or use an airtight container to store the dandelion oil in.
4. Cheesecloth or a fine sieve for straining oil
5. A cooking pot that can hold the oil jar and some water
6. Turkey baster for taking any remaining sediment off the oil

Making Dandelion Oil

Ingredients

2 cups of freshly picked dandelion flowers. *(No roots or stems)*

l cup of extra virgin olive oil *(you can also do a 50/50 blend with another oil like jojoba or avocado if you want)*

Directions

Wash off the dandelion flowers and let them dry out for a few hours. Make sure you clean off any residue dirt or leaves.

Fill the cooking pot with enough warm water to cover the lower half of the jar. Place on the stove or a burner on a low heat.

In a 12 to 15 oz sealed jar place the dandelion flowers and oil together. Use the turkey baster to remove any excess residue or water that may be on the top of the oil.

When placing the oil jar into the water, make sure your stove setting is kept on warm. Keep the oil warm in the water for 12 to 24 hours. Every few hours you will need to check the water level in the pot to ensure it remains at half full around the jar.

After the 24 hour cycle has been completed, the dandelion flowers can sit for up to one week in the oil before the final straining process.

Using the cheesecloth or sieve, slowly strain the dandelion oil into another clean sealed jar (or air tight container).

If you see any water droplets and film left in the oil, use a turkey baster to remove as it's one of the easiest ways to do this.

Used dandelion flowers can be added into a compost pile, so there's no wasting any part of this plant. Old dandelion flowers can become part of next year's crop as mulch.

Notes on shelf life

You can keep dandelion infused oil for up to 12 months in the refrigerator and it's not a hard process making the infused oil.

The extra added benefit of premixing dandelion oil means you will have it on hand when you really need it later on.

Infused Oil Shopping List

I have included alternative utensils and supplies someone may need when making the infused dandelion oil. There are a few items in this list that I did not include previously and so I thought to add them now.

I have also included a link at the bottom of this page to a website, where you can see photographs of the step-by-step process in the creation of this oil.

Sieve is needed when straining the oil.

Funnel makes life a lot easier for pouring

Spoons can come from the utensil drawer

Hot plate burner or a stove

Coffee filters alternative for oil straining

Mortar and pestle because it will help you grind up the dandelions

Double boiler or skillet

Cheesecloth (alternatives: pillowcase, flour sack or bandana)

Clean and sanitized dry glass jars (medium size)

How To Make Infused Oils:

https://www.instructables.com/id/How-to-make-Infused-Oil/

Power Juices

"As Samuel Spaulding, Esquire, once said, 'Dig in the earth, delve in the soul.' Spin those mower blades, Bill, and walk in the spray of the Fountain of Youth. End of lecture. Besides, a mess of dandelion greens is good eating once in a while." - Ray Bradbury, Dandelion Wine

Most people are not aware that you can throw a handful of dandelion leaves in juice mixes and because dandelions have dark green leaves, they are full of potent nutrients.

I have provided a couple of very simple recipes that you can put in a blender every morning. Why not try what I like to call the dandelion juice power drink. If you suffer from swollen joints or arthritis, this juice recipe can help your body fight off the oxidation process, responsible for all that pain.

In a blender at the following ingredients: One chopped up green apple, half a cucumber, two celery sticks, a handful of Dandelion leaves with a small amount of fresh lemon juice. Throw in some ice, add a little water, mix everything together well and you have a power juice drink that will provide sweetness with a load of antioxidant properties mixed in.

For people who have issues with acne, dandelions leaves combined with lemon juice will actually help the microbial bacterial infection underneath the skin. This is good news for people who are trying to cure the acne from the inside out.

About Dandelion Smoothies

If you want a thicker smoothie over a juice recipe, add in some more cucumber, celery and apple. The best part about this recipe is that you can make your own special blend. Some people become more creative by adding in herbs like cilantro into their power juice.

If you want a fruit smoothie over power juice, use a handful of dandelion greens, 1 cup of mixed berries, one banana and 1 chopped up apple (green or red). Add a little cinnamon and honey into the mix for taste. Blend all ingredients together. These drinks are a combination of taste, antioxidant properties with an energy boost. Health alternatives that offer our bodies ultimate wellbeing and they taste great too.

Were you also aware that lemonades and cordials can also be made from Dandelions?

Seriously though, is there anything this potent little plant can't do?

Dandelion Lemonade

If you like the taste of honey and lemon tea then you will love this dandelion Lemonade. This recipe consists of four basic ingredients. All you will need is warm water, honey, dandelion flowers and fresh lemon juice, that's it!

Dandelion Root Tea can replace the plain water in the lemonade recipe if you wish. I would suggest you make the tea ahead of time, and then move onto the rest of the recipe a day later.

Ingredients

- 8 cups of freshly picked Dandelion flowers
- The juice from 5 lemons
- I gallon of warm water (16 cups of water)
- 5 to 10 tablespoons of Honey depends on your desired sweetness level.

Example: For every cup of Dandelion Lemonade add in 1 to 2 teaspoons of honey to the final cup of lemonade.

Add water and lemon juice together into a large glass container or jug.

Add in warm honey (so it will blend into the lemonade) and Dandelion flowers.

Give the lemonade a stir and chill it down for 3 hours in the refrigerator.

Strain out all of the flowers and serve.

Dandelion Cordial

Ingredients

- 1.2 cups of Dandelion flower petals only *(remove the green back off the flowers)* or approximately 110 flowers.
- 1.5 cups of warm water
- 1 cup of granulated brown sugar
- 1 tablespoon of honey

Method

Mix the flower petals with the water and let sit for 24 hours.

After 24 hours strain out the petals from the water into a medium sized cooking pot. Turn on the burner to a medium heat.

Now add in the honey and sugar and continuously stir until the sugar is completely dissolved.

Bring mixture to a boil for 5 minutes while constantly stirring. Take off the heat and store in an air tight container in the fridge.

When you want to use Dandelion Cordial:

Add 16 tablespoons of the cordial into 5 cups of water.

Mix together and serve with a slice of lemon for added taste.

Wines and Mead

"What I need is the dandelion in the spring. The bright yellow that means rebirth instead of destruction. The promise that life can go on, no matter how bad our losses. That it can be good again". -Suzanne Collins

When I first started looking into beer and wine making with dandelions I was astounded to learn, making mead wasn't such a hard process at all. I was impressed with the idea that within a few weeks of making my own alcoholic beverages, I could be drinking a potent homemade brew.

Knowing that I wasn't going to be adding additives into my wine like sulfates, was all the incentive I needed to give some homemade products a try.

So in this section of the book I have also included a mead, beer, wine and vinegar recipe, which will give you plenty of homemade varieties to create and try.

Dandelion Vinegar

Dandelion vinegar can be added into salads and used in other foods during the cooking process. It's really easy to make this recipe and it can replace other recipes that call for vinegar.

Pour 1 to 2 teaspoons of dandelion vinegar over salads or pour 1 teaspoon over greens before steaming them for a little taste.

2 teaspoons in water 2 hours before meals will help people who suffer from stomach issues. This vinegar will help reduce the acid build up in the stomach and instead will create healthy gut bacteria.

Ingredients

1 cup Dandelion flowers

2 cups Apple cider vinegar

One pint sized Mason Jar with lid.

Instructions

Remove the green backs off behind the dandelion flower. Clean and dry flowers off and place in the Mason jar.

Cover flowers with apple cider vinegar. Shake the bottle everyday and store in a cool dark place.

Before using vinegar: Strain off the flowers first to use remaining vinegar.

Dandelion Mead

Mead has always been one of those liquids I wanted to try my hand at making. It's one of the oldest of alcoholic beverages we know of and the honey, gives mead a rich and wonderful flavor.

Dandelion mead like other drinks you can make from this plant will have a lemony-honey taste to it. Of course the honey will make this version of mead, something flavorful and unique to try.

I do encourage people to try and buy from local farmers who also keep bees. Local pollen is especially great for people who have allergies. Local honey can help your body adapt to allergens that come from grass pollens and other flowering fauna in the area.

Fermentation

You will need some kind of fermentor to make dandelion mead. I have linked a kit below that is easy to set up. There are all kinds of equipment you can purchase off the internet but what you chose to ferment the mead, is entirely up to you.

Actually this is a great website because it offers all kinds of different types of equipment for wine, beer and mead making. You might find something here:

https://www.homebrewing.org/Brewing-Equipment_c_133.html

Ingredients

1 Lemon (squeezed juice)

1 cup plump raisins

1 gallon of spring water

4 cups of local fresh honey

1 teaspoon of a Yeast nutrient

1 gram of Fleischmann's dry fermenting yeast (or similar yeast)

3 cups of dandelion flower petals (take all the green parts off the flowers)

Method

Collect 3 cups of Dandelion flower heads in full bloom. Remove as much of the green from the back of the flower to reduce bitterness. Rinse off petals and set to the side.

In a medium pot, boil the spring water. Add 4 cups of boiled water into a mason jar along with the petals. Place in the refrigerator and steep for 24 hours.

Remove the rest of the water off the heat and add in the honey. Stir honey in heated water until fully dissolved. Now add in the lemon juice, raisins and yeast into a pre-sanitized two gallon fermentor with the water and honey.

Seal fermentor and leave for 24 hours, until mead cools down to seventy degrees. After a day of steeping, strain dandelion petals away from the dandelion tea and add them into fermentor.

Dandelion Beer

This recipe will make ten to twelve-12-ounce bottles of beer. As with other beer sold in stores, dandelion beer will have a normal yeast taste to it but with a lovely homemade feel.

People who make their own beer actually prefer the taste to store bought because there are no sulphates or questionable shelf life additives included. Instead homemade offers peace of mind in knowing all about the ingredients we include in beer. Considering that beer and mead have some of the oldest recipes known to humanity, it stands to reason that making your own beer is a great drink to make.

I have previously supplied a link to a distributor who sells beer, wine and mead making kits and supplies. Please refer to the mead making section in this book for the appropriate link.

Always remember to sanitize your equipment before use.

Ingredients:

5 quarts of spring water

1/4 cup warm water

1 pound of raw sugar

1 cup of washed and chopped Dandelion leaves

1/2 ounce of roasted dandelion root. *Please refer to the section in this book on dandelion coffee on how to roast the root.*

1/2 ounce of fresh ginger, unpeeled and grated

1 tablespoon beer yeast or granulated bread yeast

1 ounce of cream of tartar

Method:

Place dandelion leaves and ginger root into a large cooking pot with the five quarts of spring water. On a high heat, bring the ingredients to a boil. Reduce heat to low and further simmer for another 8 to 10 minutes. This will is the main part of the brew.

Mix the yeast with the warm water in a small bowl and set the mix aside.

Place the sugar and cream of tartar into a clean fermentation container. *If you are using a homemade set-up make sure you are not using an aluminum container to brew the beer in. Instead use food grade safe plastic, pottery or a stainless steel stock pot with lid.*

Line a colander with cheesecloth or muslin cloth. Place the colander over the fermentation container (which contains the sugar and cream of tartar). Now pour the 5 quarts of dandelion water brew through the cheesecloth colander.

Stir these ingredients together while completely dissolving the sugar and let the brew cool to room temperature. Once the beer reaches room temperature (approx 70 degrees) add in the yeast mixture previously set aside.

Cover fermentation container with a small towel and sit in warm area in the home. Make sure there is no direct sunlight on the container but just enough warmth to keep the fermentation container warm for 3 to 4 days.

Stir the beer once a day during this time, while making sure all sediment is mixed around properly from the bottom of the container.

After 3 to 4 days take a funnel and place the beer into sterilized bottles. Make sure your lids are airtight.

Be careful not to scoop out the remaining sediment at the bottom of the fermenting container also known as "Lees" into the bottles.

Store the beer bottles (containers) on their side in a cool place until ready to drink. You can use the refrigerator, pantry, root cellar or basement as a place to store the beer.

Let the beer sit quietly for at least seven days before drinking however this dandelion beer recipe, will mature in about 3 weeks and will taste much better if you are prepared to wait.

Note:

The longer the beer is able to ferment the higher and quality of taste will be. Most people who make their own beer will tell you that in 2 weeks people can expect to have a light ale type of beer.

Between 4 to 6 weeks of fermenting, will create more of an old fashioned type of lager.

Dandelion Wine

This is a very easy recipe to follow and you can either make this recipe as called for or pre-make a dandelion tea and use that with this recipe. I recommend you try different tastes when it comes to dandelion wine because some people prefer a fruitier blossom taste over a dry white wine feel.

The recipe calls for 1 cup of dandelion blossoms but if you want to add more, feel free to do so. You will come to know what works better; especially if you are planning on morphing this wine into something you really want to drink.

You are looking at one hour of prep time with about fifteen minutes of cooking time. You will also need a thermometer to check water temp.

Ingredients:

1 cup of fresh dandelion blossoms *(remove the green back off all the flowers and rinse the blossoms well)*

1 gallon of boiling water

Or replace water and blossoms with a premade dandelion tea.

1 package of wine yeast

8 cups white sugar

1 fresh orange thinly sliced

1 fresh Lemon thinly sliced

Method:

Place dandelion blossoms into the boiling water and stand for five minutes.

Remove the blossoms from the water and then cool down to 90 degrees F.

Now stir in yeast, sugar, orange and lemon slices.

Pour wine into a fermentor and attach the fermentation lock.

Ferment the wine in a cool area of the home like a basement or root cellar.

Bubbling during the fermentation phase will discontinue in 10 to 14 days time. Once the bubbling has stopped you can then bottle into wine jars with air tight seals or sterilized Mason jars with seals. Strain the wine through cheesecloth before bottling to ensure there is no Lees going into the wine containers.

Remember not to use the wine at the bottom of the fermentor as it will contain Lees (remaining yeast) which will spoil the bottled wine as it ages.

Age the wine for four to six weeks for the best possible flavor.

Jams & Jellies

"If you find yourself worrying, go outside, take three breaths, address a tree and quietly say, 'Thank you.' If you can't find a tree, a dandelion will do... Nature is magic". -Robert Bateman

For anyone who likes to make homemade jellies and jams making your own is so much healthier for you than any store bought product you will buy. Most of the jellies and jams people see lined up on grocery store shelves are filled with chemicals like High Fructose Corn Syrup and other additives.

Some labels on food products and additives actually say "Natural Flavoring" now, when in fact they are bi-products from cells. Castoreum comes from a beaver's anus gland or Hek 293 flavoring is actually embryonic kidney cells? These natural flavors do sweeten the food but at what cost does humanity pay for such questionable additives from store bought products?

I strongly recommend making your own foods, jellies and juices because at least you will know exactly what was added into the ingredients.

There are mountains of different recipes off the internet now so making jelly is something anyone can do. I personally think dandelion jelly is unique because of the added health benefits that come from the plant and is now in the homemade jam.

If you like orange or lemon marmalade you will enjoy the taste of dandelion Jam. It has a strong honey taste with just a hint of lemon added into it. Bees love dandelions so the great thing about this plant is the flowers do retain a strong honey taste to any recipe you care to make.

A Dandelion Jelly Recipe

Ingredients

4 cups water

4.5 cups dandelion flower petals (yellow and white parts only)

1/4 cup pectin PLUS 2 teaspoons powdered pectin

4 - 3/4 cups granulated sugar

3 tablespoons fresh lemon juice

Method

Remove all the backs off the dandelion flowers. Use only the blossom part of the flower.

In a medium saucepan (or cooking pot) bring blossoms and water to boiling.

Reduce the heat down to medium and simmer for 4 minutes. Remove from heat, and let blossom water stand for 15 minutes.

Strain water (approximately 4 cups) through a fine sieve and into a medium bowl. Top up water levels until the mixture equals 4 cups.

Combine 1/4 cup pectin and 3/4 cup sugar together in a small bowl.

In a medium saucepan add in strained flower water along with the 1/4 cup pectin and 3/4 cup of sugar. Bring ingredients to a boil making sure the sugar is dissolved.

Slowly add in the remaining 4 cups of sugar while constantly stirring. All sugar should be completely dissolved before moving forward.

Once all the sugar is dissolved, add in the remaining pectin mixture and keep stirring until everything is smooth and all sugar has dissolved.

Add in lemon juice and boil for a further 2 minutes.

Scoop the foam off the surface of jelly mixture with a spoon and let jelly cool for about 15 minutes.

While the jelly is still warm add ingredients into airtight containers or mason jars.

Refrigerate for about 4 hours before using.

Creative Foods

"If dandelions were hard to grow, they would be most welcome on any lawn". -Andrew Mason

There are so many different creative foods anyone can create from harvesting dandelions. I have already shown you homemade products like beer, mead, vinegar, jams and salves but were you aware that you can also bake cookies and cakes with dandelions?

There are all kinds of recipes that call for dandelion greens in recipes like pesto and pasta. Because the leaves have a slight bitter taste to them, dandelion leaves can be made into an ideal salad dressing.

Why not create some dandelion vinegar *(recipe supplied in this book)* add in some granulated garlic with Italian herbs and you have a quick and easy salad dressing to use on the dinner table.

Cakes and cookies can also be made from dandelions. Just as people will use carrots and zucchini in cake and bread recipes, dandelion flowers and leaves can be used to make all kinds of creative foods.

Dandelion Vanilla Cookies

Ingredients:

1 cup virgin almond oil (or virgin olive oil)

1/2 cup local honey

2 eggs

1.5 teaspoons vanilla extract

1 cup dry oatmeal

1 cup unbleached organic flour (or replace with almond or coconut flour)

1/2 cup dandelion petals (take the green off the back of the flower)

Method:

Pre-grease a cookie sheet tray

Preheat the oven to 375 degrees F.

Put the blender on a slow to medium setting and mix the almond oil and honey together. Now add in the two eggs and vanilla, continue to mix.

Now turn the blender down to a low setting and fold in the flour, oatmeal and dandelion flowers. Make sure the batter is completely mixed together.

Add the batter onto the pre-greased cookie sheet tray.

Use one dessertspoon full of batter and press down onto the cookie tray with a fork. Leave a space between each cookie and bake for 10-15 minutes. Cool cookies down before serving.

Dandelion Lotions & Salves

"No creature is fully itself till it is, like the dandelion, opened in the bloom of pure relationship to the sun, the entire living cosmos". -D. H. Lawrence

I know I have mentioned this previously but dandelions can make amazing soaps, lotions and moisturizing salves for all kinds of skin treatments. If you want beautiful skin, then try a homemade dandelion lotion or soap.

I really want to encourage people to become involved in the making of more natural products because skills like these are not only a dying art form, but homemade products are much healthier on the body.

Making your own soaps and lotions is especially beneficial especially if you if you have a child or elderly person at home who is constantly suffering from skin rashes and other skin conditions.

Some of these allergic reactions could be coming from store bought products that contain a lot of chemical additives in them. Some of these so called gentle products have nasty chemicals like formaldehyde and parabens in them, so is it any wonder our skin is becoming more allergic.

Homemade products such as soaps, lotions, bars and chap sticks will contain natural oils like coconut and almond oil. Virgin oils cold pressed oils have natural healing enzymes that help to soothe dry irritated skin.

Apart from creating personal care products such as lipbalm you can also make a dandelion shave balm to soothe dry skin along with other items like tinctures and shampoo. The possibilities are endless with this amazing little plant.

Coconut oil is another natural main ingredient found in all kinds of soaps and lotions. This oil adds an extra protective layer over the skin with its antimicrobial properties to help protect the skin from infections. When coconut oil is added in with dandelion salves and lotions we end up with a product that protects, soothes and repairs external problems on and inside the body.

Other oils such as almond, jojoba and olive oil moisturize and help to repair damage done to skin, hair and nails. So you see making your own body products is highly beneficial for everyone in the family.

From babies to the elderly homemade dandelion skin care products have the family health care program covered.

Other Useful Info About Soap Making

I felt it was necessary to add a small section in this book about some of the processes you will come across during soap making. If you've never made soap before and start reading about **Trace** in soap, you have to be wondering what that actually means, so I included a few little pointers I know will help make the process easier.

For example: fancy soap molds are lovely to have but if you are going to be making soap for the family a simple square mold work just as well. Unless you are planning on making soaps and lotions as gifts for the Holiday Season or as a birthday gift, you don't need to spend money to purchase anything other than simple molds.

Soap Dyes

If you have decided on using a natural dye for soap making, then you should know natural dyes do not have all those bright colors you would see on commercially made soaps.

A natural dye will look lighter with milder colors and will have less allergic side effects on the skin.

Some of the allergic side effects someone may be experiencing from using soap could be coming from the bright colored dyes used in the manufacturing process. Some artificial dyes also contain other toxic residues and why it pays to check into the ingredients first. You will find the link below very helpful, especially if you are considering a natural dye to colorize soap.

Source: https://www.diynatural.com/natural-soap-colorants/

What Is Trace In Soap Making

Trace is when you see the oils, butter, water and lye melding together. It's during this time when you can add in essential oils like tea tree, lemon, lavender, vanilla or orange for extra added fragrance. Trace is also the time when food coloring can also be added into the soap.

The Cold Soap Making Process

The cold process of soap making is highly recommended for these recipes. To learn how to make the cold processing method, please connect to the link below especially if you are new to soap making. The reason why we prefer to use the cold process is because it doesn't damage any of the healing proteins and acids found in oils like coconut and jojoba oil.

Cold processing ensures oils still retain their maximum health benefits. If you have inflammation problems like arthritis, making dandelion soap can actually help the muscles with swelling. Best of all there is peace of mind in knowing there are no toxic ingredients added into the soap making process.

Source: https://www.soapqueen.com/bath-and-body-tutorials/cold-process-soap/free-beginners-guide-to-soapmaking-cold-process/

I am providing you with a couple of natural soap recipes so you can try your hand at making some Dandelion soap. I have also provided a shopping list of products that you will find at the end of the soap making recipes.

Dandelion Lavender Soap

This soap is made from dandelions and coconut oil but has also had essential oils such as lavender and orange added in for extra fragrance. Lavender makes us feel relaxed and soothed while the orange essential oil makes us feel invigorated and refreshed.

Ingredients:

8 oz dandelion infused oil *(Please see section on creating homemade Dandelion oil)*

8.5 oz water *(or replace water for dandelion tea)*

3.5 oz lye

0.35 oz lavender essential oil

0.20 oz orange essential oil

7 oz coconut oil

3oz Shea butter

3 oz cocoa butter

2.5 oz castor oil

0.20 oz Natural soap making dye *(see link below)*

Source: https://www.brambleberry.com/colorants-c181.aspx

Method

Combine all oils and butter together in a medium sized bowl. Mix all ingredients together in a blender on slow speed. Now slowly add in the water and lye and continue mixing the soap.

Stop the blender and use a spatula to check for any air bubbles in the mix. Go back to blending on a low speed.

Continue mixing soap until most of the bubbles are gone and the soap reaches trace. This will happen when all the oils, butter dandelion tea and lye has emulsified.

Once you are satisfied with the fragrance and color of the soap, pour into molds. Make sure you tap around the sides of each mold and remove any extra air bubbles.

Keep the Dandelion Soap in the mold for up to 48 hours before removing.

If you are using a larger mold cut soap bar into sections and let it cure for 4 to 6 weeks.

Dandelion Jojoba Soap

All ingredients are in ounces and milliliter measurements. Soap is measured by weight. **Remember:** Once soap reaches trace, you can then add in color or other fragrance into the mixture.

Ingredients:

10 oz (300 ml) premade Dandelion Tea.

(Find the dandelion tea recipe in this book)

4 oz   (120 ml) Lye

14 oz (420 ml) Virgin Olive Oil

8 oz   (240 ml) Virgin Coconut Oil

1.5 oz (45 ml)   Jojoba Oil

1.5 oz (45 ml)   Tamanu Oil

3oz   (90ml)   Sunflower Oil

2oz   (60 ml) Shea Butter

Method:

Make sure the tea is cooled down first because we will be using the tea in place of water and dandelion flowers.

Combine all oils and butter together in a medium sized bowl. Mix oil ingredients together in a blender on slow speed, check sides of bowl.

Slowly add in the dandelion tea water and lye, continue mixing the soap. Stop the blender and use a spatula to check for any air bubbles.

Continue mixing soap on a low speed until most of the bubbles are gone and the soap reaches trace. This will happen when all the oils, butter dandelion tea and lye has emulsified.

Once you are satisfied with the fragrance and color of the soap, pour into molds. Make sure you tap around the sides of each mold and remove any extra air bubbles.

Keep the Dandelion Soap in the mold for up to 48 hours before removing.

If you are using a larger mold cut soap bar into sections and let it cure for 4 to 6 weeks.

Shopping List For Soap Making

Goggles and rubber gloves.

Teaspoons and small sieve.

Soap molds and a strainer with a funnel.

Candy making thermometer or a laser thermometer.

Heavy duty plastic or rubber spatulas. Avoid aluminum or metal.

Large containers for mixing the soap. Can be plastic or glass.

Immersion hand blender (Cuisinart CSB-76W SmartStick 200-Watt)

Weighing scale because the oils, liquids and lye should only be weighed and not measured.

Disposable containers for mixing up the Lye. Avoid using glass containers because the Lye will heat up and the glass will become too hot for touching.

Dandelion Skin Lotion-Bars

These skin lotion bars will benefit people with dry skin and rashes as cold pressed virgin coconut oil contains an ingredient called lauric acid. This acid treats dry skin while the antimicrobial properties help the body fight off bacterial infections. Dandelion skin lotions bars can help the body fight inflammation which is great for people who have arthritis, fibromyalgia and swollen joints.

Ingredients:

1/2 cup beeswax

1/4 cup pure shea butter

1/4 cup virgin cold pressed coconut oil

2 teaspoons dandelion infused oil *(see infused oil recipe in this book)*

Method:

Combine the beeswax, Shea butter, coconut oil, and dandelion infused oil in a double boiler pot and heat over a low heat. ***Never heat any of these oils over any direct heat as the beneficial enzymes found in the oils can be damaged.***

Stir oils together slowly until everything is melted. The beeswax will take the longest time to melt and should be done in 15 minutes. Once everything is melted, remove from heat and pour ingredients into ice-cube molds and let them sit until completely cool which can take up to 4 hours.

The skin lotion bars should easily come out of the mold as needed.

Dandelion Lip Balm

The numerous products anyone can make from Dandelions is endless as you have read throughout this book. Below I have included this amazing lipbalm recipe which will come in handy during those cold windy days.

Ingredients:

4 Tablespoons of dried out dandelion flowers

4 tablespoons of coconut oil or olive oil

1.5 Tablespoons beeswax

Containers for Lip balm (either tubes or small pots with lids)

Method:

In a double boiler pot, melt the oils together on a low heat. Add in the dandelions and cover. Slowly stir the dandelion into the oil.

Simmer the oil on a low heat for 25 to 30 minutes. Turn off the heat and keep the pot covered. Allow the dandelions to sit overnight in the oil as the potency increases, the longer flowers are kept in the oil.

Next Day: Using a strainer separate the flowers from the oil. This means re-heating the oil on low. Add in the beeswax and stir until completely melted. It will take about ten minutes for all the beeswax to melt on a low to medium heat.

While the lip balm liquid is still warm, fill up the container pots and do not move until completely cooled in 4 to 5 hours.

Dandelion Hand Lotion

One of the best reasons to make your own products is learning about the ingredients on what is classified as natural and organic. I recommend you only use cold pressed, virgin oils and use vitamin capsules that have not been synthesized.

Ingredients

1/4 cup of dandelion-infused oil

¼ cup of sweet almond oil

½ cup distilled water

9 grams beeswax

5 grams vitamin E oil (organic not synthetic)

12 drops essential oil (Tea Tree or Lavender) for antibacterial and soothing properties

1 teaspoon rosehip seed oil (cold-pressed virgin seed oil)

1 teaspoon vegetable glycerin

Instructions

You will need a measuring scale for this recipe...

Place a small bowl on the scale accounting for the weight of the bowl and making sure it is at zero grams. Add the beeswax into the bowl until the scale reaches 9 grams in weight.

On a VERY LOW HEAT: In a small saucepan *(you can also use a double boiler pot for melting the wax and oils together),* add in the almond and dandelion infused oil together. Now add in the beeswax and slowly melt all ingredients together.

Take the saucepan off the heat and add n the vitamin E, rosehip seed oil, glycerin and essential oils.

Take your blender and pour the lotion straight into the container part. Place in the refrigerator until the lotion is fairly solid. You do not want the lotion to be as hard as a brick but just enough cool down time, so that it becomes a semi thick cream.

Turn the blender on a medium- high setting and very slowly add in the rosehip seed oil, distilled water and vegetable glycerin. Using a rubber spatula, clean down the sides of the container to ensure the consistency is even.

You can use a hand mixer if this makes the process easier but please note, the lotion will be more prone to separation after a few weeks if you take any short cuts during the processing. Store the lotion in a sterilized glass jar. To keep the lotion firm is it recommended to keep in the refrigerator.

To ensure you do not contaminate the lotion, use a clean spoon or the end of a butter knife to remove from the jar. Never use your fingers because whether you realize this or not, fingers may contain bacteria on them which could cause an eventual bacteria to form inside the lotion and primarily why I suggest using a clean metal instrument.

Final Thoughts

"I have lost my smile, but don't worry. The dandelion has it". -Nhat Hanh

How true the above quote is about dandelions. Even though you may have lost your smile today, the humble dandelion will still be around tomorrow teaching us the health benefits of this amazing plant.

As you have come to learn there are so many different ways to enjoy dandelions. You can put the leaves in a smoothie, boil up a cup of coffee from the roots and make a cake or cookies.

You can drink the flowers down in wines and mead or create soaps and lotions to heal tired and dry skin. This plant has just about everything going for it and yet for most people dandelions are still considered weeds.

Learning more about natures natural plant benefits will ensure a longer happier life.

From reading this book you now understand how important our connection is to nature, especially if we wish to have strong bones and muscles well into our 60's and 70's.

There isn't anything Mother Nature didn't include in the book of growing and well being for us to use. There are so many other plants on this planet that deserve recognition too especially for the amount of healing they also offer to humanity. However I thought by introducing you to the humble dandelion, the desire to learn more would lead you down the path into wonderful natural discoveries.

It seems like it's taken an eternity for humanity to realize that natural living and eating is definitely best lifestyle for the human body, mind and spirit.

Wishing you all the best in future dandelion adventures.

Stay happy and healthy

Connie McCauley

Stay Updated On New Books

Being healthy is really important to my family and I'm sure it is to yours too. Writing books about natural plant extracts such as Dandelions was important for me because I am an avid supporter of nature's bounty.

I also see a great lack of understanding about our current food system and the connection to nature's bounty. This book was designed to bring people closer to everything that can be seen with the eye, while at the same time, teaching us to be more conscious of the delicate eco system. As you have learned from this book, there are many different ways someone can easily become more self-sufficient by using natural plant based alternatives such as Dandelions.

I would like to encourage people to read my other book about eating more natural foods over store bought products. Ditch The Diets gives people a great idea of where our food should come from and why eating natural foods means never gaining weight again.

Source:
https://www.amazon.com/author/conniemccauley

 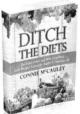

Manufactured by Amazon.ca
Acheson, AB